CALENDAR ART

upper left, Aztec day; *upper right,* Mayan month; *lower left,* Babylonian star; *lower right,* Egyptian solar disc

CALENDAR ART

Thirteen days, weeks, months,
and years from around the world

WRITTEN AND ILLUSTRATED BY
LEONARD EVERETT FISHER

FOUR WINDS PRESS   NEW YORK

This one is for Marge, too.

Four Winds Press
Macmillan Publishing Company
866 Third Avenue, New York, NY 10022
Collier Macmillan Canada, Inc.
First Edition
Printed in the United States of America

10 9 8 7 6 5 4 3 2 1

The text of this book is set in 12 pt. Trump.
The illustrations are rendered in pen-and-ink and scratchboard.

Library of Congress Cataloging-in-Publication Data
Fisher, Leonard Everett.
Calendar art.
Summary: Discusses what various civilizations have done
to measure time. Includes Aztec, Babylonian, Roman, and more.
1. Calendar   [1. Calendar]   I. Title.
CE11.F57 1987   529.3   86-25835
ISBN 0-02-735350-8

CALENDAR ART

200-YEAR CALENDAR 1850–2050

1851	1857	1852*	1853	1854	1855	1850
1856*	1863	1858	1859	1865	1860*	1861
1862	1868*	1869	1864*	1871	1866	1867
1873	1874	1875	1870	1876*	1877	1872*
1879	1885	1880*	1881	1882	1883	1878
1884*	1891	1886	1887	1893	1888*	1889
1890	1896*	1897	1892*	1899	1894	1895
1902	1903	1909	1898	1905	1900	1901
1913	1908*	1915	1904*	1911	1906	1907
1919	1914	1920*	1910	1916*	1917	1912*
1924*	1925	1926	1921	1922	1923	1918
1930	1931	1937	1927	1933	1928*	1929
1941	1936*	1943	1932*	1939	1934	1935
1947	1942	1948*	1938	1944*	1945	1940*
1952*	1953	1954	1949	1950	1951	1946
1958	1959	1965	1955	1961	1956*	1957
1969	1964*	1971	1960*	1967	1962	1963
1975	1970	1976*	1966	1972*	1973	1968*
1980*	1981	1982	1977	1978	1979	1974
1986	1987	1993	1983	1989	1984*	1985
1997	1992*	1999	1988*	1995	1990	1991
2003	1998	2004*	1994	2000*	2001	1996*
2008*	2009	2010	2005	2006	2007	2002
2014	2015	2021	2011	2017	2012*	2013
2025	2020*	2027	2016*	2023	2018	2019
2031	2026	2032*	2022	2028*	2029	2024*
2036*	2037	2038	2033	2034	2035	2030
2042	2043	2049	2039	2045	2040*	2041
	2048*		2044*	2051	2046	2047
			2050			

Month letters (non-leap)

JAN	D	E	F	G	A	B	C
FEB	G	A	B	C	D	E	F
MAR	G	A	B	C	D	E	F
APR	C	D	E	F	G	A	B
MAY	E	F	G	A	B	C	D
JUN	A	B	C	D	E	F	G
JUL	C	D	E	F	G	A	B
AUG	F	G	A	B	C	D	E
SEP	B	C	D	E	F	G	A
OCT	D	E	F	G	A	B	C
NOV	G	A	B	C	D	E	F
DEC	B	C	D	E	F	G	A

Month letters for leap years (JAN and FEB)

JAN	C	D	E	F	G	A	B
FEB	F	G	A	B	C	D	E

Calendar letters

A

SU	MO	TU	WE	TH	FR	SA
1	2	3	4	5	6	7
8	9	10	11	12	13	14
15	16	17	18	19	20	21
22	23	24	25	26	27	28
29	30	31				

B

SU	MO	TU	WE	TH	FR	SA
	1	2	3	4	5	6
7	8	9	10	11	12	13
14	15	16	17	18	19	20
21	22	23	24	25	26	27
28	29	30	31			

C

SU	MO	TU	WE	TH	FR	SA
		1	2	3	4	5
6	7	8	9	10	11	12
13	14	15	16	17	18	19
20	21	22	23	24	25	26
27	28	29	30	31		

D

SU	MO	TU	WE	TH	FR	SA
			1	2	3	4
5	6	7	8	9	10	11
12	13	14	15	16	17	18
19	20	21	22	23	24	25
26	27	28	29	30	31	

E

SU	MO	TU	WE	TH	FR	SA
				1	2	3
4	5	6	7	8	9	10
11	12	13	14	15	16	17
18	19	20	21	22	23	24
25	26	27	28	29	30	31

F

SU	MO	TU	WE	TH	FR	SA
					1	2
3	4	5	6	7	8	9
10	11	12	13	14	15	16
17	18	19	20	21	22	23
24	25	26	27	28	29	30
31						

G

SU	MO	TU	WE	TH	FR	SA
						1
2	3	4	5	6	7	8
9	10	11	12	13	14	15
16	17	18	19	20	21	22
23	24	25	26	27	28	29
30	31					

*LEAP YEAR LETTERS

To find a specific day: (1) Locate the year. (2) In the same column below, find the letter for the month; use bottom JAN and FEB for *leap years. (3) Match the month letter to the calendar letter on the right.

DAYS, WEEKS, MONTHS, AND YEARS

Throughout the existence of humankind, people have been aware of the special rhythms of the sun and the moon. Primitive humans saw that the sun rose in one place, turning night into day, and that it set in another place, turning day into night. To them the moon, too, seemed to emerge from one position, move across the star-strewn sky, and disappear with the night at another position. They believed, then, that each day and each night the sun and the moon traveled an endless, repetitive course.

In others words, early people thought that the earth stood still as heavenly objects circled around it. Their knowledge was limited in this way from the dawn of the human epoch, about 500 thousand years ago, until about 440 years ago. It was then that the astronomer Nicolaus Copernicus (1473–1543) offered a startling idea: that the sun stood still, that the earth was one of a group of heavenly bodies moving around it, and that as the earth moved in a measurable orbit around the sun, the moon traveled around the earth in its own measurable path.

Whatever the limits of early people's knowledge of the heavens, they knew there was a passage of time—from sunrise to sunset. And they knew that aging, growing from young to old, was a process of time. While they did not measure a day in seconds, minutes, and hours, they knew when it began and ended, and that it took 365¼ days for the sun to appear and disappear at identical positions—a solar year. Early people knew, too, that in some mysterious way the position of the sun determined the seasons.

The moon also provided a broad measure of timekeeping for these people. In the darkness they watched the moon change from no shape at all—the invisible new moon—to a slim crescent, a half moon, an oval, or *gibbous*, a full moon, then back to a gibbous, half-moon, and crescent, before it became the shadowy new moon again. These phases of the moon always spanned 29½ days. This was the length of time it took the moon to orbit the earth once—the lunar month.

Our word *month* derives from *moon*. Early people knew that 12 lunar months nearly equaled one solar year, falling short by about 11 days. And as civilization evolved, people realized that they had to try to compensate for those days. A rough estimate of nature's timing was no longer good enough. People needed a chart to tell them with certainty when to plant and harvest their crops, when to work, and when to pray. They needed a time-measuring system—a calendar.

The Greek and Roman civilizations gave us the word *calendar*. Its roots are in the Greek *kalend*, "I shout," and in the Roman *calends*, the first day of a Roman month. The ancient Greek who shouted *kalend* was a public timetable who informed the people when to pay their taxes, when the magistrates would try criminals, and when marketing days and religious and athletic events would take place. Other cultures—Aztec, Chinese, Jewish, Moslem—used varying systems to calculate days, weeks, months, and years. There was no standard calendar in use anywhere in the ancient world. And most of these systems, if not all, were based on either the lunar month or the solar year.

The ancient Sumerians devised the first lunar calendar about 5,000 years ago. Later, Babylonians divided months into weeks and a week into 7 days. The Jews, once captive in Babylonia, used the Babylonian 7-day week, as did the sun-worshiping Egyptians, who developed a 52-week solar calendar based on the 7-day week.

The schemes were too complicated, however, and calendar dates and seasons became mismatched. The problem worsened each year. Farmers could not rely on these calendars to plant crops. Religious celebrants never knew the right day for a particular festival. Fall weeks of one year would become winter weeks the next year.

Julius Caesar (circa 100–44 B.C.) tried to adjust the calendar so that it would repeat itself the same way every year. Progress was made, but not enough. Then early Christians modified Caesar's "Julian" calendar so that all years following year 1, when Jesus Christ was born, would be known as A.D., or *anno domini*, "in the year of the Lord," and those that came before as B.C., before Christ, or B.C.E., before the common era. Still, calendar errors continued to multiply.

Finally, Pope Gregory XIII (1502–1585) corrected the calendar. Now its dates would conform year after year to the proper seasons with almost no error. The "Gregorian" calendar continues to be the calendar of our modern world.

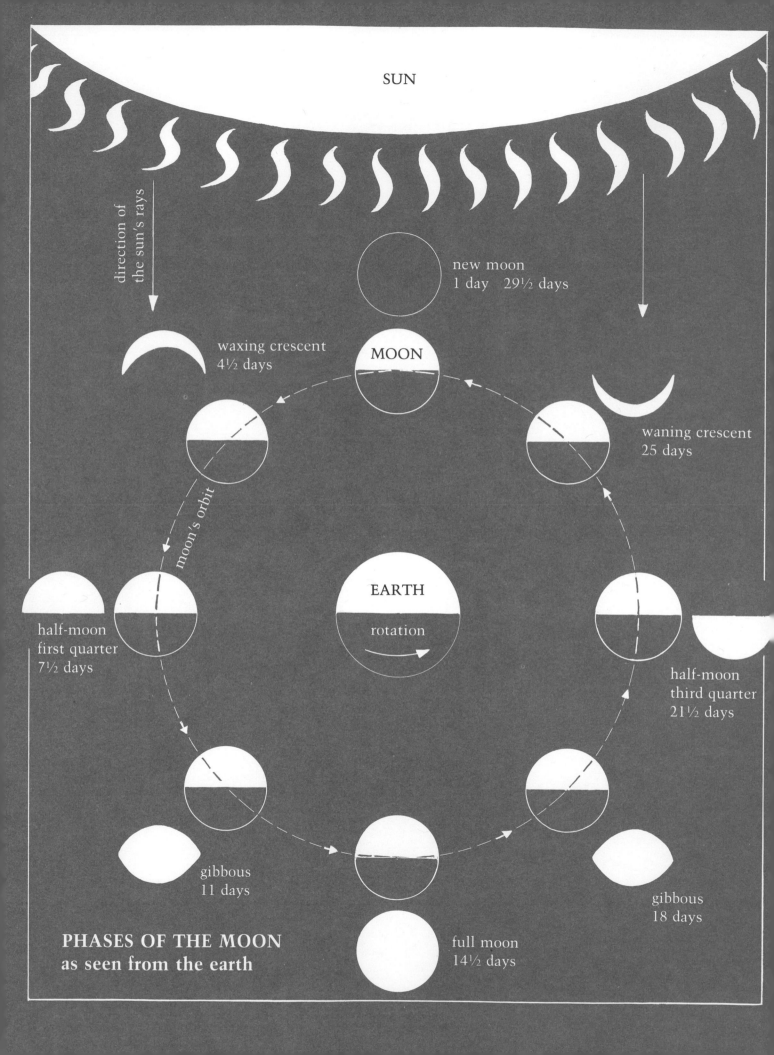

SUN

direction of the sun's rays

new moon
1 day   29½ days

MOON

waxing crescent
4½ days

waning crescent
25 days

moon's orbit

EARTH

rotation

half-moon
first quarter
7½ days

half-moon
third quarter
21½ days

gibbous
11 days

gibbous
18 days

PHASES OF THE MOON
as seen from the earth

full moon
14½ days

THE CALENDARS

AZTEC

BABYLONIAN

CHINESE

EGYPTIAN

FRENCH REVOLUTIONARY

GREGORIAN

HEBREW

ISLAMIC

JULIAN

MAYAN

ROMAN

STONEHENGE

WORLD

AZTEC

Tenochtitlan—now Mexico City—was the capital of the Aztec empire when Spanish adventurer Hernando Cortez (1485–1547) first saw it in 1519. This busy center of 100 thousand people was a surprising place to the Spaniards, who had come from Europe to bring civilization to the Americas. Built on a lake, Tenochtitlan was a city of canals, bridges, causeways, aqueducts, brick houses, and great decorative pyramid temples. It was run by an organized government based on religion and headed by priests. Presiding over this society, one of the most powerful and civilized in Central America, stood a king-emperor, resplendent in the golden glitter his exalted position required. In Cortez's day he was Montezuma II (1480–1520).

The Aztec nation emerged at the end of 3,000 years of human development in Central America. And Aztec power, warring and mystically religious—they tore the beating hearts out of human sacrificial victims—savaged the people for a 200-year period (circa 1320–1520), until they were conquered by the Spaniards. But what was most remarkable about the Aztecs was their ability to run their lives by a complex written calendar derived from the nearly precise computations of the movement of the sun, moon, and stars.

Based on a 365-day solar year, the Aztec calendar consisted of 18 months, each having 20 days, plus an additional 5 days to complete the year. Within these 365 days was a special group of 260 days that formed a religious calendar. The calendar worked for 52 years before the seasons no longer matched. Unable to correct the mismatch, the Aztecs started a new calendar for another 52-year cycle.

AZTEC SOLAR YEAR

No.	Modern Dates	Aztec Year Names	Aztec Month Names	Aztec Day Names
1	Feb 12–Mar 3		Atlcoualco	Cipactli (Crocodile)
2	Mar 4–Mar 23		Tlacaxipeualiztli	Ehecatl (Wind)
3	Mar 24–Apr 12	I. Calli (House)	Tozoztontli	Calli (House)
4	Apr 13–May 2		Huei Tozoztli	Cuetzpallin (Lizard)
5	May 3–May 22		Toxcatl	Coatl (Snake)
6	May 23–Jun 11		Etzalqualiztli	Miquiztli (Skull)
7	Jun 12–Jul 1		Tecuhilhuitontli	Mazatl (Deer)
8	Jul 2–Jul 21	II. Tochtli (Rabbit)	Hueitecuhilhuitl	Tochtli (Rabbit)
9	Jul 22–Aug 10		Tlaxochimaco	Atl (Water)
10	Aug 11–Aug 30		.Xocotlhuetzi	Itzcuintli (Dog)
11	Aug 31–Sept 19		Ochpaniztli	Ozomatli (Monkey)
12	Sep 20–Oct 9		Teotleco	Malinalli (Grass)
13	Oct 10–Oct 29	III. Acatl (Reed)	Tepeilhuitl	Acatl (Reed)
14	Oct 30–Nov 18		Quecholli	Ocelotl (Ocelot)
15	Nov 19–Dec 8		Panquetzaliztli	Cuauhtli (Eagle)
16	Dec 9–Dec 28		Atemoztli	Cozcaquauhtli (Vulture)
17	Dec 29–Jan 17		Tititl	Ollin (Earthquake)
18	Jan 18–Feb 6	IV. Tecpatl (Knife)	Izcalli	Tecpatl (Knife)
19	Feb 7			Quiauitl (Rain)
20	Feb 8			Xochitl (Flower)
	Feb 7–Feb 11	Nemontemi (the "5 useless days")		

AZTEC DAY SIGNS

1
CIPACTLI
crocodile

2
EHECATL
wind

3
CALLI
house

4
CUETZPALLIN
lizard

5
COATL
snake

6
MIQUIZTLI
skull

7
MAZATL
deer

8
TOCHTLI
rabbit

9
ATL
water

10
ITZCUINTLI
dog

11
OZOMATLI
monkey

12
MALINALLI
grass

13
ACATL
reed

14
OCELOTL
ocelot

15
CUAUHTLI
eagle

16
COZCAQUAUHTLI
vulture

17
OLLIN
earthquake

18
TECPATL
knife

19
QUIAUITL
rain

20
XOCHITL
flower

BABYLONIAN

About 3000 B.C., long before the Greeks named the hot desert region between the Tigris and Euphrates rivers Mesopotamia, "the land between rivers," nomadic tribes quit wandering and formed farming towns. Chief among these towns was Ur, located on the banks of the Euphrates River at the northern rim of the Persian Gulf. The area was called Sumer. To help them deal with the dry land, the Sumerian farmers relied on their priest-astronomers to interpret the movement of the stars. They developed a 30-day lunar calendar and used it to plan their farming. These same Sumerians invented the first writing system, *cuneiform*. With it came the beginning of history: the written record.

Ur and the Sumerians faded after a 700-year presence. Babylon—the biblical Babel—and Babylonians arose in their place. However, during the kingdom of Hammurabi, circa 1750 B.C., a revised Sumerian calendar emerged as a Babylonian calendar.

The Babylonians devised a 354-day lunar calendar with 12 alternating months of 29 and 30 days. But it fell 11¼ days short of the 365¼-day solar year. To correct the calendar so that the seasons matched their dates somewhat each year, they *intercalated*, or "inserted," two extra months seven times within every 19-year period. Also, the Babylonians were among the first civilizations to divide their year into 7-day weeks. The Babylonian week was based solely on the worship of the sun, moon, and five planets: Shamash (Sun/Sunday), Sin (Moon/Monday), Nebo (Mercury/Tuesday), Ishtar (Venus/Wednesday), Nergal (Mars/Thursday), Marduk (Jupiter/Friday), and Ninurta (Saturn/Saturday).

BABYLONIAN SKY SYMBOLS

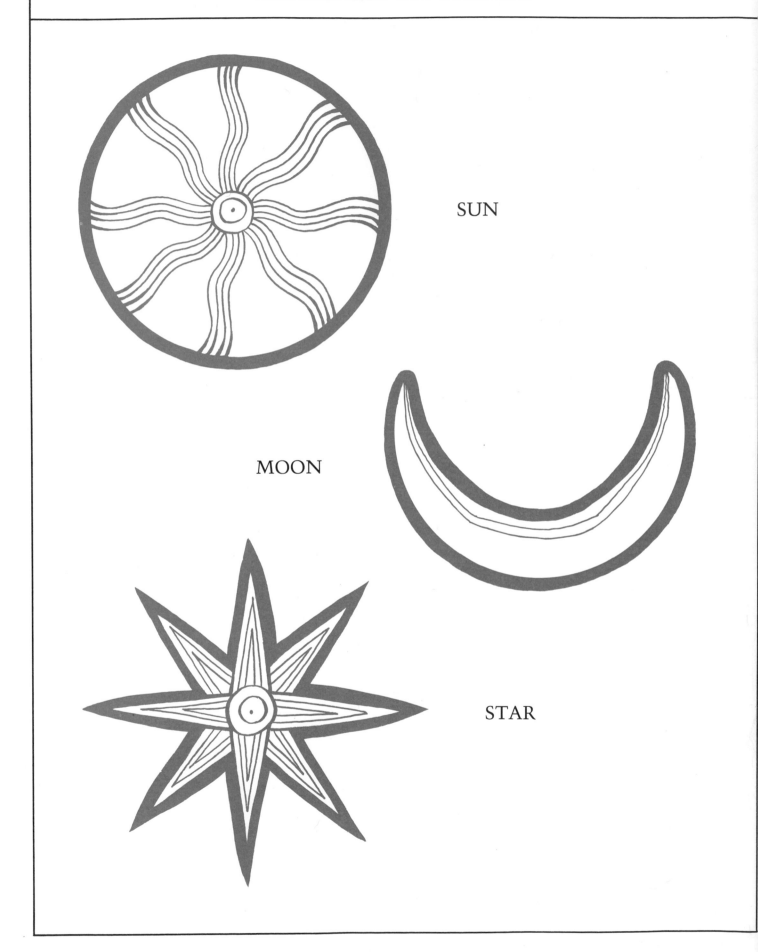

SUN

MOON

STAR

BABYLONIAN MONTHS

⟨ 1.	⟨⟨ 2.	⟨⟨⟨ 3.
NISANU	AIARU	SIMANU
⟨⟨⟨ 4.	⟨⟨⟨ 5.	⟨⟨⟨ 6.
DUZU	ABU	ULULU
⟨⟨⟨ 7.	⟨⟨⟨ 8.	⟨⟨⟨ 9.
TASHRITU	ARAHSAMNU	KISLIMU
⟨ 10.	⟨⟨ 11.	⟨⟨⟨ 12.
TEBETU	SHABATU	ADDARU

Intercalated months: ULULU II (29 days)   ADDARU II (30 days)

CHINESE

The Chinese is the oldest continuous civilization in the world. Although its written history began with the Hsia dynasty 4,192 years ago, the Chinese calendar, the oldest continuously used calendar in the world, predated Chinese written history and the Hsia. According to Chinese folklore, a mythical ruler, Huang Ti, invented the calendar in the first year of his reign—2698 B.C. (by Western reckoning)—to help farmers plant and harvest at the right seasons. That year became the first year of Chinese time. Therefore, our year 1987 + 2698 = the Chinese year 4685, the Year of the Hare.

Like other ancient calendar makers, including the Babylonians, Chinese astronomers divided their 354-day lunar year into 12 months having 29 or 30 days. They kept their calendar in line with the 365¼-day solar year by intercalating. The calendar was repeated in 60-year cycles. Within these cycles were 5 cycles containing 12 years each. Each of the 12 years was named after an animal, and the year of a particular animal occurred every 12 years. For example, the year 4600 was the Year of the Tiger, and the next Year of the Tiger was 4612. While every new moon signaled a new month, each new year began when a new moon was closest to the constellation Aquarius—sometime between January 20 and February 18 on the Gregorian calendar.

Modern China uses the Gregorian calendar to run its everyday affairs. Yet the ancient, traditional lunar-solar calendar still determines the Chinese New Year and other special Chinese events.

CHINESE TRADITIONAL YEARS for the period 1902–2021

THE YEAR OF THE TIGER

4600	1902	4660	1962
4612	1914	4672	1974
4624	1926	4684	1986
4636	1938	4696	1998
4648	1950	4708	2010

THE YEAR OF THE HARE

4601	1903	4661	1963
4613	1915	4673	1975
4625	1927	4685	1987
1637	1939	4697	1999
4649	1951	4709	2011

THE YEAR OF THE DRAGON

4602	1904	4662	1964
4614	1916	4674	1976
4626	1928	4686	1988
4638	1940	4698	2000
4650	1952	4710	2012

THE YEAR OF THE SNAKE

4603	1905	4663	1965
4615	1917	4675	1977
4627	1929	4687	1989
4639	1941	4699	2001
4651	1953	4711	2013

THE YEAR OF THE HORSE

4604	1906	4664	1966
4616	1918	4676	1978
4628	1930	4688	1990
4640	1942	4700	2002
4652	1954	4712	2014

THE YEAR OF THE SHEEP

4605	1907	4665	1967
4617	1919	4677	1979
4629	1931	4689	1991
4641	1943	4701	2003
4653	1955	4713	2015

THE YEAR OF THE MONKEY

4606	1908	4666	1968
4618	1920	4678	1980
4630	1932	4690	1992
4642	1944	4702	2004
4654	1956	4714	2016

THE YEAR OF THE ROOSTER

4607	1909	4667	1969
4619	1921	4679	1981
4631	1933	4691	1993
4643	1945	4703	2005
4655	1957	4715	2017

THE YEAR OF THE DOG

4608	1910	4668	1970
4620	1922	4680	1982
4632	1934	4692	1994
4644	1946	4704	2006
4656	1958	4716	2018

THE YEAR OF THE PIG

4609	1911	4669	1971
4621	1923	4681	1983
4633	1935	4693	1995
4645	1947	4705	2007
4657	1959	4717	2019

THE YEAR OF THE RAT

4610	1912	4670	1972
4622	1924	4682	1984
4634	1936	4694	1996
4646	1948	4706	2008
4658	1960	4718	2020

THE YEAR OF THE OX

4611	1913	4671	1973
4623	1925	4683	1985
4635	1937	4695	1997
4647	1949	4707	2009
4659	1961	4719	2021

Blue numerals indicate Chinese years. Black numerals indicate Western years.

The years indicated in black are derived from the Gregorian calendar.

The years indicated in blue are derived from the ancient Chinese calendar.

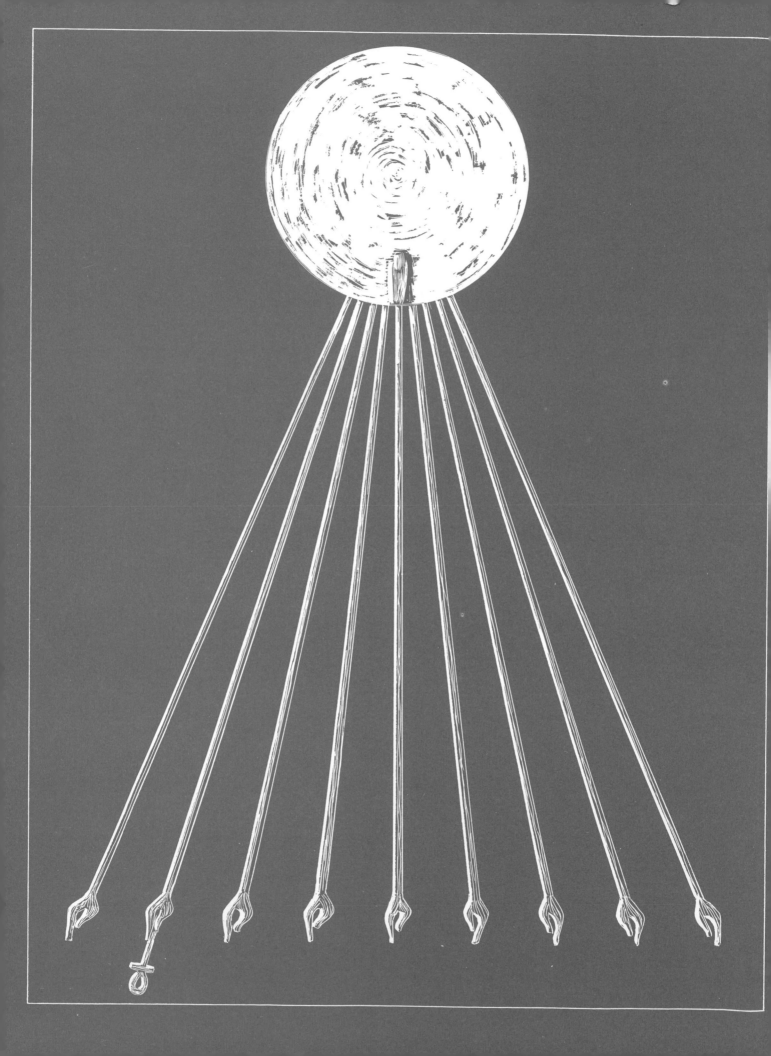

EGYPTIAN

An object of ancient worship, the Nile River is the spirit and lifeblood of Egypt. For without that great wash of water flowing from Ethiopia to the Mediterranean Sea, Egypt would be a desert. Once each year for the past 5,000 years of Egyptian recorded time, the Nile has flooded the 600-mile-long valley to create a green and fertile tract for planting.

Early Nile Valley farmers had to know when the river would flood in order to save their crops, their property, and even their lives. They knew that the flooding would begin whenever the brightest fixed star, Sirius (Sothis to the Egyptians), rose on the eastern horizon. This took place about once every 365 days, just before sunrise. So they developed a lunar calendar in which a year began with the first new moon following the appearance of Sirius. The lunar calendar year, containing 12 months with 29½ days each, covered 354 days, 11 short of 365. To make sure the flooding of the Nile and the calendar date always matched, they added an extra month every so often.

In time the Egyptians created a more accurate 360-day solar calendar with 12 months of 30 days each, along with the 7-day week favored by Jews and Babylonians. Since this, too, fell short, they added 5 days to the last month of the year. Of course, Egyptian astronomers knew that a year was 365¼ days long. But their priests, guardians of centuries of tradition, forbade them to correct the calendar by adding an extra day every four years—a leap year. Eventually the calendar fell out of line with the seasonal flooding.

ANCIENT EGYPTIAN MONTHS (named after Egyptian gods)

WINTER

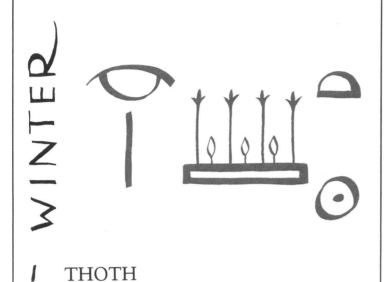

1   THOTH

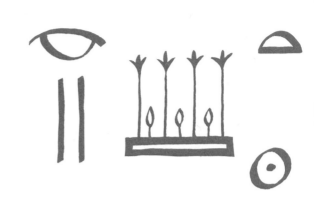

2   PAOPI

SPRING

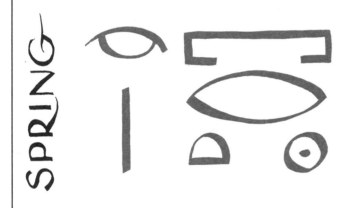

1   TOBI

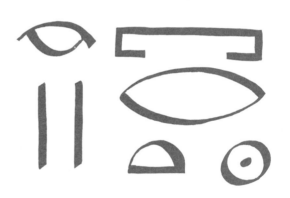

2   MEKHIR

SUMMER

1   PAKHON

2   PAONI

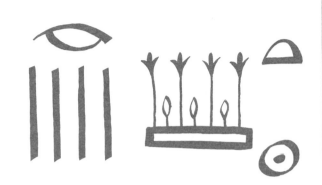

3 HATHOR

4 KHOIAK

3 PHAMENOTH

4 PHARMUTHI

3 EPEP

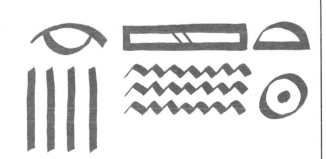

4 MESORE

FRENCH
REVOLUTIONARY

On September 20, 1792, the French National Convention met in Paris to frame a new constitution. For four years France had been torn by revolution and by war with Austria and Prussia. Two days later, September 22, the National Convention ended the monarchy and declared itself a republic. Seven years later, in 1799, the agony of France ended—but not before a reign of terror had bloodied the country and changed its social order.

To emphasize the complete change in French affairs and to show their hatred for everything that hinted of the monarchy, including the Catholic Church, the revolutionaries abolished the Gregorian calendar, the timetable of the Western world. In its place they put the French Revolutionary calendar.

Sundays and all religious holidays, like Christmas, were deleted from the new calendar. The year began on September 22, the date of the establishment of the republic. It consisted of 12 months, as always. However, each of the 12 months, now renamed, contained 30 days. Five additional days were intercalated to complete a 365-day cycle. These were the *Sans Culottides*, "without knee pants," so-called in honor of the revolutionary working-class men who wore trousers. In addition, the calendar was divided into 36 weeks, each having 10 days. The days had numerical names: *Primidi, Duodi, Tridi, Quartidi, Quintidi, Sextidi, Septidi, Octidi, Nonidi, Decadi.* The 10-day groups were called *Decades*. Every tenth day was a rest day, and the *Sans Culottides* were rest days, too. The new calendar was short lived. On January 1, 1806, Napoleon Bonaparte abolished it and restored the Gregorian calendar.

FRENCH REVOLUTIONARY CALENDAR 1793–1805

Months Days	VENDEMIAIRE (Fine Wine) September–October			BRUMAIRE (Fog) October–November			FRIMAIRE (Frost) November–December		
Duodi	22	2	12	22	2	12	22	2	12
Tridi	23	3	13	23	3	13	23	3	13
Quartidi	24	4	14	24	4	14	24	4	14
Quintidi	25	5	15	25	5	15	25	5	15
Sextidi	26	6	16	26	6	16	26	6	16
Septidi	27	7	17	27	7	17	27	7	17
Octidi	28	8	18	28	8	18	28	8	18
Nonidi	29	9	19	29	9	19	29	9	19
Decadi	30	10	20	30	10	20	30	10	20
Primidi	1	11	21	1	11	21	1	11	21

	NIVOSE (Snow) December–January			PLUVIOSE (Rain) January–February			VENTOSE (Wind) February–March		
Duodi	22	2	12	22	2	12	22	2	12
Tridi	23	3	13	23	3	13	23	3	13
Quartidi	24	4	14	24	4	14	24	4	14
Quintidi	25	5	15	25	5	15	25	5	15
Sextidi	26	6	16	26	6	16	26	6	16
Septidi	27	7	17	27	7	17	27	7	17
Octidi	28	8	18	28	8	18	28	8	18
Nonidi	29	9	19	29	9	19	29	9	19
Decadi	30	10	20	30	10	20	30	10	20
Primidi	1	11	21	1	11	21	1	11	21

FESTIVAL OF THE REVOLUTION DAY occurred once every fourth, or "leap," year. Each four-year period was named a FRANCIADE.

Months / Days	GERMINAL (Seed) March–April			FLOREAL (Flower) April–May			PRAIRIAL (Meadow) May–June		
Duodi	22	2	12	22	2	12	22	2	12
Tridi	23	3	13	23	3	13	23	3	13
Quartidi	24	4	14	24	4	14	24	4	14
Quintidi	25	5	15	25	5	15	25	5	15
Sextidi	26	6	16	26	6	16	26	6	16
Septidi	27	7	17	27	7	17	27	7	17
Octidi	28	8	18	28	8	18	28	8	18
Nonidi	29	9	19	29	9	19	29	9	19
Decadi	30	10	20	30	10	20	30	10	20
Primidi	1	11	21	1	11	21	1	11	21

	MESSIDOR (Harvest) June–July			THERMIDOR (Heat) July–August			FRUCTIDOR (Fruit) August–September		
Duodi	22	2	12	22	2	12	22	2	12
Tridi	23	3	13	23	3	13	23	3	13
Quartidi	24	4	14	24	4	14	24	4	14
Quintidi	25	5	15	25	5	15	25	5	15
Sextidi	26	6	16	26	6	16	26	6	16
Septidi	27	7	17	27	7	17	27	7	17
Octidi	28	8	18	28	8	18	28	8	18
Nonidi	29	9	19	29	9	19	29	9	19
Decadi	30	10	20	30	10	20	30	10	20
Primidi	1	11	21	1	11	21	1	11	21

VIRTU	(Virtue)		1
GENIE	(Genius)		2
TRAVAIL	(Labor)	SANS CULOTTIDES	3
OPINION	(Opinion)		4
RECOMPENSE	(Reward)		5

Pope Gregory XIII

GREGORIAN

By the sixteenth century, errors in the Julian calendar had become a problem for the Catholic Church. Easter was supposed to be celebrated on the vernal equinox, the day the sun crosses the equator, turning winter into spring in the Northern Hemisphere, summer to fall in the Southern Hemisphere. And the vernal equinox was supposed to occur on the first Sunday after the first full moon after March 21. But March 21 had moved 10 days ahead of the equinox. While the vernal equinox would occur every 365¼ days, as usual, March 21 would soon be in midsummer.

Pope Gregory XIII ordered the calendar changed to correct the errors. After ten years of study, the Pope decreed that October 5, 1582, would become October 15, 1582, to bring the dates into line with the sun's position. Ten days were dropped from the calendar. Also, though January 1 would continue to be New Year's Day, leap year would no longer be any year divisible by four. While a leap year still would occur every four years by adding one day to February, the last year of a century could not be a leap year unless it was divisible by 400. The year 1900, for example, could not be a leap year. The year 2000 would be a leap year. Now it would be 30,000 years before the calendar would become 10 days out of line.

It took two hundred years for Protestant Europe, namely, England and Germany, to accept the Gregorian calendar. The Russians did not adopt it until 1918. Moslems, Jews, and Greek Orthodox people continue to use their own ancient calendars for religious events. But the business of nearly the entire modern world is conducted by the Gregorian calendar.

DAYS OF THE WEEK AROUND THE MODERN WORLD

ENGLISH	MEANING	ORIGINS
Sunday	Sun Day	
Monday	Moon Day	
Tuesday	Tiw's Day	Tiw was the war god in German mythology, the counterpart of the Roman god or planet, Mars.
Wednesday	Woden's Day	Woden was the messenger god in German mythology, the counterpart of the Roman god or planet, Mercury.
Thursday	Thor's Day	Thor was the supreme god in German mythology, the counterpart of the Roman god or planet, Jupiter.
Friday	Frigg's Day	Frigg was the love goddess in German mythology, the counterpart of the Roman goddess or planet, Venus.
Saturday	Saturn Day	

ENGLISH	LATIN	FRENCH	SPANISH	ITALIAN	DANISH	DUTCH
Sunday	Dominus God	Dimanche	Domingo	Domenica	Soendag	Zondag
Monday	Dies Lunae Moon's Day	Lundi	Lunes	Lunedi	Mandag	Maandag
Tuesday	Dies Martis Mars's Day	Mardi	Martes	Martedi	Tirsdag	Dienstag meeting day
Wednesday	Dies Mercurii Mercury's Day	Mercredi	Miercoles	Mercoledi	Onsdag	Woensdag Woden's day
Thursday	Dies Jovis Jupiter's Day	Jeudi	Jueves	Giovedi	Torsdag	Donderstag thunder day
Friday	Dies Veneris Venus's Day	Vendredi	Viernes	Venerdi	Fredag	Freitag
Saturday	Dies Saturni Saturn's Day	Samedi	Sabado sabbath	Sabato sabbath	Loerdag bath day	Zaterdag

GREGORIAN CALENDAR FOR THE YEAR 2000 (A LEAP YEAR)

JANUARY

Su	Mo	Tu	We	Th	Fr	Sa
						1
2	3	4	5	6	7	8
9	10	11	12	13	14	15
16	17	18	19	20	21	22
23	24	25	26	27	28	29
30	31					

FEBRUARY

Su	Mo	Tu	We	Th	Fr	Sa
		1	2	3	4	5
6	7	8	9	10	11	12
13	14	15	16	17	18	19
20	21	22	23	24	25	26
27	28	29				

MARCH

Su	Mo	Tu	We	Th	Fr	Sa
			1	2	3	4
5	6	7	8	9	10	11
12	13	14	15	16	17	18
19	20	21	22	23	24	25
26	27	28	29	30	31	

APRIL

Su	Mo	Tu	We	Th	Fr	Sa
						1
2	3	4	5	6	7	8
9	10	11	12	13	14	15
16	17	18	19	20	21	22
23	24	25	26	27	28	29
30						

MAY

Su	Mo	Tu	We	Th	Fr	Sa
	1	2	3	4	5	6
7	8	9	10	11	12	13
14	15	16	17	18	19	20
21	22	23	24	25	26	27
28	29	30	31			

JUNE

Su	Mo	Tu	We	Th	Fr	Sa
				1	2	3
4	5	6	7	8	9	10
11	12	13	14	15	16	17
18	19	20	21	22	23	24
25	26	27	28	29	30	

JULY

Su	Mo	Tu	We	Th	Fr	Sa
						1
2	3	4	5	6	7	8
9	10	11	12	13	14	15
16	17	18	19	20	21	22
23	24	25	26	27	28	29
30	31					

AUGUST

Su	Mo	Tu	We	Th	Fr	Sa
		1	2	3	4	5
6	7	8	9	10	11	12
13	14	15	16	17	18	19
20	21	22	23	24	25	26
27	28	29	30	31		

SEPTEMBER

Su	Mo	Tu	We	Th	Fr	Sa
					1	2
3	4	5	6	7	8	9
10	11	12	13	14	15	16
17	18	19	20	21	22	23
24	25	26	27	28	29	30

OCTOBER

Su	Mo	Tu	We	Th	Fr	Sa
1	2	3	4	5	6	7
8	9	10	11	12	13	14
15	16	17	18	19	20	21
22	23	24	25	26	27	28
29	30	31				

NOVEMBER

Su	Mo	Tu	We	Th	Fr	Sa
			1	2	3	4
5	6	7	8	9	10	11
12	13	14	15	16	17	18
19	20	21	22	23	24	25
26	27	28	29	30		

DECEMBER

Su	Mo	Tu	We	Th	Fr	Sa
					1	2
3	4	5	6	7	8	9
10	11	12	13	14	15	16
17	18	19	20	21	22	23
24	25	26	27	28	29	30
31						

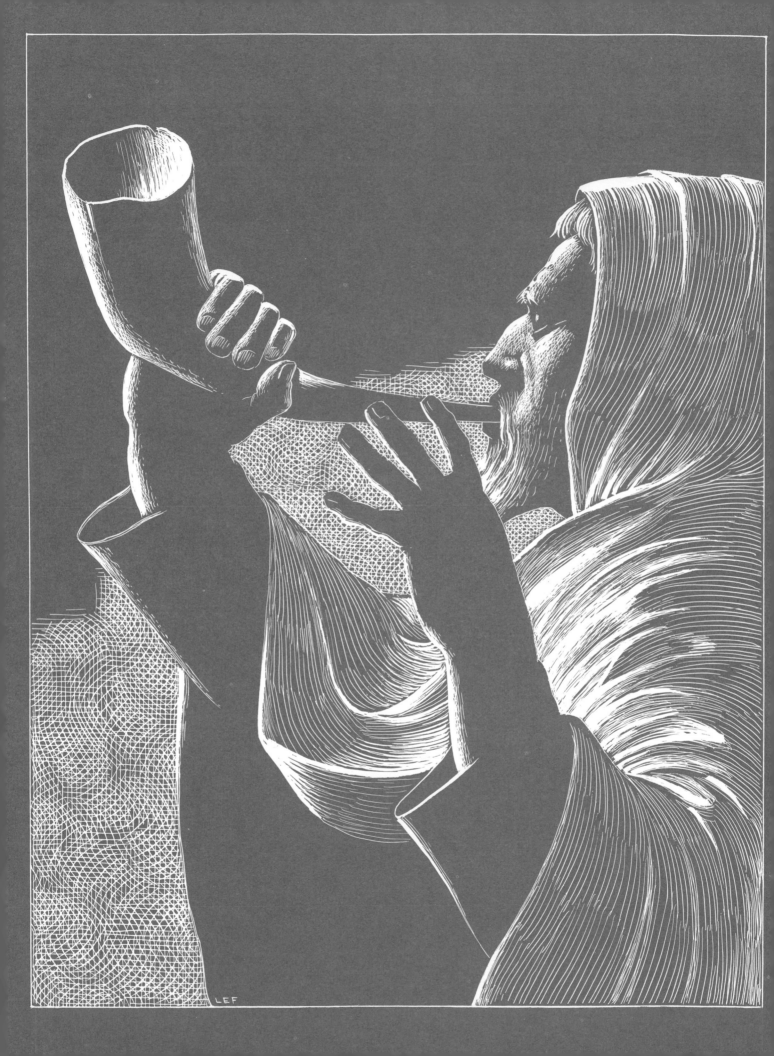

HEBREW

According to Jewish tradition, the world began in the fall of 3761 B.C. Thus, September 24, 1987, on the Gregorian calendar begins the Jewish year 5748 (1987 + 3761 = 5748).

For a long time, the Hebrew, or Jewish, calendar was based on the lunar month. Not until they were dragged into captivity by the Babylonians in 586 B.C.—about 650 years after Moses had led them out of Egypt—did the Jews fit the sun's position to their moon calculations and formulate a luni-solar calendar like the Babylonians'. When the Jews returned to Judea in 538 B.C., they brought with them the Babylonian 7-day week; a 24-hour day that began at sunset; the Babylonian *Sabattu* (the Hebrew *Shabbat*, or "day of rest"); and the Babylonian months. They also introduced the Babylonian signs of the zodiac to the region. In addition, they used the Babylonian New Year, which began in the autumn month of *Tashritu* (*Tishri* in Hebrew), and a calendar whose 29- or 30-day months had to be adjusted by adding 7 extra months during every 19-year period to keep pace with the sun's seasonal positions. Even the solar year had to be adjusted every 28 years because holy events could not fall on certain days of the week. The holiest day, Yom Kippur, the Day of Atonement, could never occur on either the first or sixth weekday, Sunday or Friday, for example. Even the Jewish New Year had to begin on a particular day of the week. Such rules forced the Jewish calendar into years having 353, 354, 355, or 383, 384, and 385 days. Despite the complications, the Jewish calendar is still used by the world's religious Jews and the State of Israel.

JEWISH YEAR showing important holidays Months shown in ( ) are Babylonian

1

TISHRI

(Tashritu)

September–October

30 days

Day
1: Rosh Hashanah
(New Year)

10: Yom Kippur
(Day of Atonement)

15–22: Succoth
(Feast of Tabernacles)

23: Simhat Torah
(Rejoicing in the Law)

2

חשבן

CHESHVAN

(Arahsamnu)

October–November

29 or 30 days

3

כסלו

KISLEV

(Kislimu)

November–December

29 or 30 days

Day
25: Hanukkah
(Festival of Lights)

4

TEVETH

(Tebetu)

December–January

29 days

5

SH'VAT

(Shabatu)

January–February

30 days

6

ADAR

(Addaru)

February–March

29 days

Day
14: Purim
(Delivery of the Jews in
Persia)

7

נִיסָן

NISAN

(Nisanu)

March–April

30 days

Day

15–22: Pesach
(Passover)

8

אִייָר

IYAR

(Aiaru)

April–May

29 days

9

סִיוָן

SIVAN

(Simanu)

May–June

30 days

Day

6: Shavuoth
(Festival of the Ten
Commandments)

10

תַמוז

TAMUZ

(Duzu)

June–July

29 days

11

אָב

AV

(Abu)

July–August

30 days

Day

9. Tishah B'Av
(Commemoration of the
Destruction of the First
and Second Temples)

12

אֱלוּל

ELUL

(Ululu)

August–September

29 days

ISLAMIC

The idol-worshipping people of Mecca in southwestern Arabia had had enough of Mohammed the Prophet (570–632), who had been preaching that there was only one god, Allah. On Friday, July 16, 622, Mohammed had to flee for his life. He continued his teaching at Yathrib, now the city of Medina. When he died ten years later, his preaching had already sparked what would become one of the world's most persuasive religions—Islam—with some 500 million believers. Mohammed's flight, called the Hegira, would become the most meaningful event to his followers, the Moslems.

A few years after Mohammed's death, the Moslem world was introduced to a new calendar that used the Hegira as its starting point. It was a lunar calendar that fixed the Islamic year at 354 days. Within that year were 12 months having 29 and 30 days alternately. Each month began with the official sighting of the crescent of the new moon. There were 7-day weeks as well, to which a day was added when required to reach the fixed figure of 354. Of course, since it was 11¼ days short of the 365¼-day solar year, the Islamic calendar was always moving backward in time. To correct the misalignment, extra days were added periodically, including one additional day during a leap year.

Like the Jews, Moslems began and ended their day at sundown. But they did it chiefly because Mohammed had entered Yathrib at sundown. And because he had entered it on the Moslem sabbath, *el Jumah*, this is the only day of the week to have a standard name. Also, it is the first day of the week. Corresponding to the Gregorian Friday, *el Jumah* is considered the day of the Hegira. The Islamic calendar is still the religious calendar of the entire Moslem world.

ISLAMIC YEAR

1	2	3
مُحَرَّم	صفر	ربيع الأوّل
MUHARRAM	**SAFAR**	**RABI I**
30 days	29 days	30 days
Day 1–10: Fast of Yom Ashoora		Day 12: Mohammed's Birthday Feast
4	5	6
ربيع الثّاني	جمادى الأوّل	جمادى الثّاني
RABI II	**JUMADA I**	**JUMADA II**
29 days	30 days	29 days
Day 12: el Hoseyn's Birthday Feast (Mohammed's Son)		

7	8	9
دجب	شعبان	رمضان
RAJAB	**SHA'BAN**	**RAMADAN**
30 days	29 days	30 days
Day 12: Mohammed-Goes-to- Heaven Feast (Ascension in 632)		Day 1–30: Fast of Ramadan

10	11	12
شوّال	ذو القعده	ذو الحجّه
SHAWWAL	**DHU AL-QADA**	**DHU AL-HIJJAH**
29 days	30 days	29 days
Day 1–3: Feast of Eed el Sagheer (Breaking of the Fast, or The Small Feast)		(1 extra day is added at intervals to fit the year to the moon's 29½-day orbit) Day 10–13: Feast of Eed el Keeber (The Sacrifice of Abraham)

Julius Caesar

JULIAN

When Julius Caesar became the Roman ruler in 49 B.C., the 355-day, 12-month Roman calendar was several months out of line with the 365¼-day solar year. Holidays meant to be celebrated in *Aprilis*, the second month, were now falling in *Sextilis*, the sixth month. Some effort was made to reform the calendar, but it was not successful. Roman priests and politicians fought over which month should start the new year. *Martius* was the traditional starting month, originally tied to spring planting. But farmers paid little attention to tradition because *Martius* no longer fell where it was supposed to. Politicians preferred *Januarius* because their terms of office began on the first of that month.

Caesar asked Sosigenes, a Greek astronomer, to construct a new calendar based on a 365¼-day solar year. Sosigenes added 90 days to the year 46 B.C., creating a 445-day year. Months and seasons were back where they belonged. Following that, to try to prevent future calendar drift, each year would begin in *Januarius*. Three years would have 365 days, and in every fourth year *Februarius* would have an extra day to make a 366-day leap year.

After Julius Caesar was assassinated in 44 B.C., the seventh month, *Julius* (July), was named for him. His successor, Augustus, rearranged the number of days in each month and named the eighth month after himself: *Augustus* (August). Improved but still imperfect, the Julian calendar began to show growing error over the next 300 years because the leap years were not properly observed.

JULIAN CALENDAR MONTHS DURING THE REIGN OF AUGUSTUS
(27 B.C.–A.D. 14)

I. JANUARIUS (January)

named for Janus, god of the gates

II. FEBRUARIUS (February)

named for Februus, god of cleansing one's sins

III. MARTIUS (March)

named for Mars, god of war

IV. APRILIS (April)

from the Latin *aperire*, "to open," or "to bud"

V. MAIUS (May)

named for Maia, goddess of plant growth

VI. JUNIUS (June)

from the Latin *junores*, "young people"

VII. JULIUS (July)

named for Julius Caesar

VIII. AUGUSTUS (August)

named for Augustus

IX. SEPTEMBER (September)

from the Latin *septem*, "seven"; the seventh month in earlier calendars

X. OCTOBER (October)

from the Latin *octo*, "eight"; the eighth month in earlier calendars

XI. NOVEMBER (November)

from the Latin *novem*, "nine"; the ninth month in earlier calendars

XII. DECEMBER (December)

from the Latin *decem*, "ten"; the tenth month in earlier calendars

JULIAN CALENDAR DURING THE REIGN OF AUGUSTUS (27 B.C.–A.D. 14)

C = Calends, 1st day; N = Nones, 5th or 7th day; I = Ides, 13th or 15th day;
* = 1 extra day every 4 years

JANUARIUS

I	II	III	IV	V	VI	VII
C	2	3	4	N	6	7
8	9	10	11	12	I	14
15	16	17	18	19	20	21
22	23	24	25	26	27	28
29	30	31				

FEBRUARIUS

I	II	III	IV	V	VI	VII
			C	2	3	4
N	6	7	8	9	10	11
12	I	14	15	16	17	18
19	20	21	22	23	24	25
26	27	28	*			

MARTIUS

I	II	III	IV	V	VI	VII
			C	2	3	4
5	6	N	8	9	10	11
12	13	14	I	16	17	18
19	20	21	22	23	24	25
26	27	28	29	30	31	

APRILIS

I	II	III	IV	V	VI	VII
						C
2	3	4	N	6	7	8
9	10	11	12	I	14	15
16	17	18	19	20	21	22
23	24	25	26	27	28	29
30						

MAIUS

I	II	III	IV	V	VI	VII
	C	2	3	4	5	6
N	8	9	10	11	12	13
14	I	16	17	18	19	20
21	22	23	24	25	26	27
28	29	30	31			

JUNIUS

I	II	III	IV	V	VI	VII
				C	2	3
4	N	6	7	8	9	10
11	12	I	14	15	16	17
18	19	20	21	22	23	24
25	26	27	28	29	30	

JULIUS

I	II	III	IV	V	VI	VII
						C
2	3	4	5	6	N	8
9	10	11	12	13	14	I
16	17	18	19	20	21	22
23	24	25	26	27	28	29
30	31					

AUGUSTUS

I	II	III	IV	V	VI	VII
		C	2	3	4	N
6	7	8	9	10	11	12
I	14	15	16	17	18	19
20	21	22	23	24	25	26
27	28	29	30	31		

SEPTEMBER

I	II	III	IV	V	VI	VII
					C	2
3	4	N	6	7	8	9
10	11	12	I	14	15	16
17	18	19	20	21	22	23
24	25	26	27	28	29	30

OCTOBER

I	II	III	IV	V	VI	VII
C	2	3	4	5	6	N
8	9	10	11	12	13	14
I	16	17	18	19	20	21
22	23	24	25	26	27	28
29	30	31				

NOVEMBER

I	II	III	IV	V	VI	VII
			C	2	3	4
N	6	7	8	9	10	11
12	I	14	15	16	17	18
19	20	21	22	23	24	25
26	27	28	29	30		

DECEMBER

I	II	III	IV	V	VI	VII
					C	2
3	4	N	6	7	8	9
10	11	12	I	14	15	16
17	18	19	20	21	22	23
24	25	26	27	28	29	30
31						

MAYAN

Mexico's Yucatan Peninsula and present-day Honduras and Guatemala were once the lands of the Maya. Long before Europeans arrived in the Western Hemisphere during the 1500s, the Mayan Indians had achieved a distinctive civilization. Their large cities—Copan, Chichen Itza, Tikal, and others—were administered by priests whose writings and astronomical observations, carved in stone or set down on tree-bark paper, provided a record of history, science, medicine, and religion, including human sacrifice. The priest-astronomers had developed a precise numbering system to manage Mayan lives at least 300 years before the birth of Christ, some 2,300 years ago. It enabled them precisely to measure planetary movements, time, and eclipses, and to develop a calendar for religious and civil affairs.

Mayan dating indicates that an accurate solar calendar was in use by them early in the common era in Europe, about the year 300. The Maya relied on two calendars working together in 52-year cycles called the *xiuhmolpilli*. One was the *haab*, a 365-day civil calendar having 18 months of 20 days each, plus a nineteenth month of 5 days. An extra day was added every fourth year. The 18-month period was called a *tun*. Twenty tuns were a *katun*. The other was a religious calendar, or *tzolkin*, having 260 sacred days.

The Maya did not have a written language that expressed sound. Instead, like the Egyptians, they used symbols called *hieroglyphs*, or *glyphs*, to express an idea. And they used a variety of number, word, and name glyphs to work out their calendar and convey its meaning.

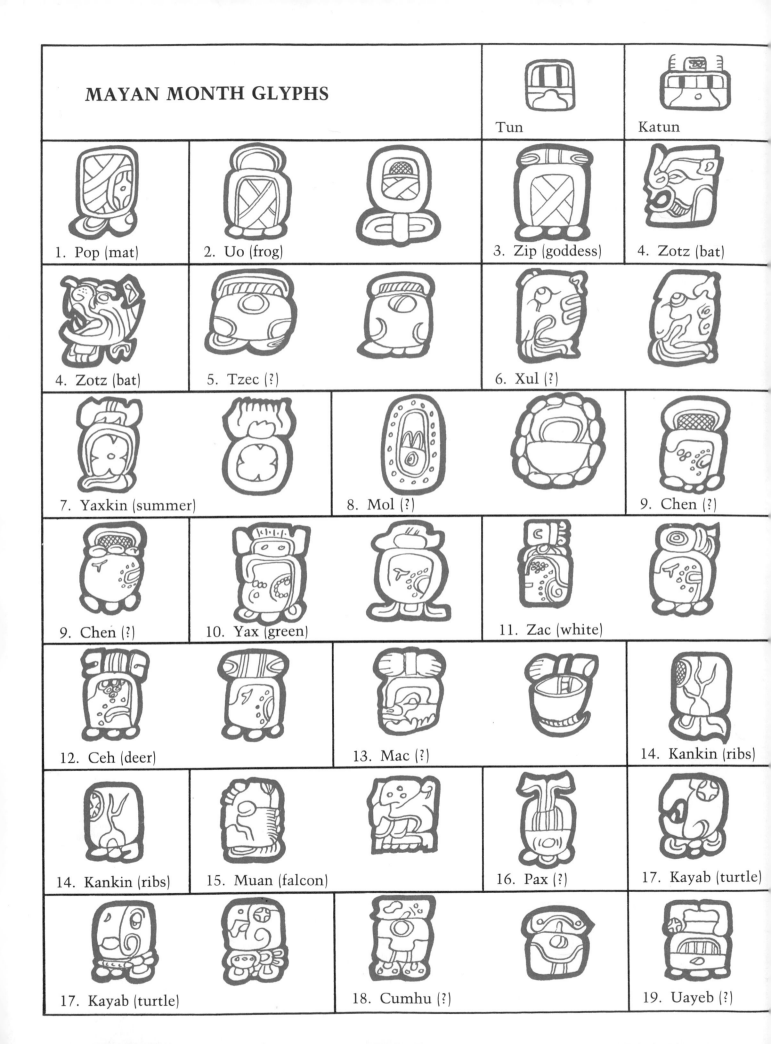

MAYAN MONTH GLYPHS

Tun

Katun

1. Pop (mat)

2. Uo (frog)

3. Zip (goddess)

4. Zotz (bat)

4. Zotz (bat)

5. Tzec (?)

6. Xul (?)

7. Yaxkin (summer)

8. Mol (?)

9. Chen (?)

9. Chen (?)

10. Yax (green)

11. Zac (white)

12. Ceh (deer)

13. Mac (?)

14. Kankin (ribs)

14. Kankin (ribs)

15. Muan (falcon)

16. Pax (?)

17. Kayab (turtle)

17. Kayab (turtle)

18. Cumhu (?)

19. Uayeb (?)

MAYAN DAY GLYPHS

Tzolkin

Haab

Kin (day)

1. Imix (water)

2. Ik (air)

3. Akbal (night)

4. Kan (corn)

5. Chicchan (serpent)

6. Cimi (death)

7. Manik (deer)

8. Lamat (rabbit)

9. Muluc (rain)

10. Oc (dog)

10. Oc (dog)

11. Chuen (monkey)

12. Eb (broom)

12. Eb (broom)

13. Ben (reed)

14. Ix (jaguar)

15. Men (eagle)

16. Cib (owl)

17. Caban (earth)

18. Eznab (knife)

19. Cauac (storm)

20. Ahau (lord)

ROMAN

Roman history claims that the Roman calendar was invented in 753 B.C., when Rome was founded. Credit for both the calendar and the founding is given to the legendary King Romulus. Descendants of the Trojan Aeneas, Romulus and his brother, Remus, were abandoned as babies and nursed by a she-wolf.

Romulus's solar year began at the spring equinox. It consisted of 305 days having 10 months of 30 and 31 days. The first month of the New Year was *Martius.* Since Romulus thought the calendar was 60 days short of a solar year, he intercalated 60 extra days throughout the year to make up the difference. But the solar year is 365¼ days. Romulus's calendar lost one day every four years. In 120 years, the calendar would fall a month behind. *Martius* would be in the wrong season. *Aprilis* would have slipped into its place.

Romulus's successor, Rome's second king, Numa Pompilius, tried to improve the calendar. He added two more months, *Januarius* and *Februarius,* and divided the 12 months into seven 29- and four 31-day periods, plus one 28-day period (*Februarius*). The day count now formed a 355-day year. Still short, this time by 10¼ days, Numa's calendar would be putting its dates next to the wrong seasons, too, albeit at a slower pace than Romulus's calendar. Again, days were inserted to make up the difference. But too often, too many days were intercalated. Numa's calendar became unreliable.

CALENDAR OF ROMULUS circa 753 B.C.

I **MARTIUS**	II **APRILIS**
(March) 31 days	(April) 30 days
III **MAIUS**	IV **JUNIUS**
(May) 31 days	(June) 30 days
V **QUINTILIS**	VI **SEXTILIS**
(fifth) 31 days	(sixth) 30 days
VII **SEPTEMBER**	VIII **OCTOBER**
(seventh) 30 days	(eighth) 31 days
IX **NOVEMBER**	X **DECEMBER**
(ninth) 30 days	(tenth) 31 days

CALENDAR OF NUMA POMPILIUS circa 715 B.C.

I MARTIUS 31 days	**II** APRILIS 29 days	**III** MAIUS 31 days
IV JUNIUS 29 days	**V** QUINTILIS 31 days	**VI** SEXTILIS 29 days
VII SEPTEMBER 29 days	**VIII** OCTOBER 31 days	**IX** NOVEMBER 29 days
X DECEMBER 29 days	**XI** JANUARIUS 29 days	**XII** FEBRUARIUS 28 days

STONEHENGE

The movement of the sun along the horizon is tracked by an arithmetical system, or calendar, that determines when the year begins, ends, and begins again. The calendar also orders the months and days within the year, based on the time it takes the moon to orbit the earth. And humans have devised various mechanical means for recording their calendars: scratch marks in dirt, bark or paper writing, stone carving, woodcarving, printing, and more. Though not exactly a record, one of the most unusual and mysterious devices used to observe the change of seasons is the great circle of stones called Stonehenge that sits on the Salisbury Plain in southwestern England. It comprises two circles of stone, within which are two half circles. At the center curve of the inner half circle is the flat Altar Stone. Beyond the outer circle is a single stone, the Heel Stone. The entire structure is nearly 100 feet in diameter and some 30 feet high. Several of the stones weigh 50 tons. They were brought to this spot from distant Wales at the end of the Stone Age, 4,000 years ago.

We do not know who erected the stones or why. What we do know is that at sunrise in midsummer, June 21–24, the longest days of the year, one can stand at the Altar Stone and watch the sun rise directly over the Heel Stone, casting a long shadow across the Altar Stone. In the evening in midwinter, December 21–24, the shortest days of the year, one can stand at the Altar Stone and watch the moon rise between two tall inner-circle stones that frame the Heel Stone. There is a seeming calendar function in the connection between the sky and the stones. It indicates that ancient Britons were driven by their worship of the heavens to construct a stone device, or temple, to keep track of the seasons.

POSSIBLE ORIGINAL PLAN OF STONEHENGE circa 2000 B.C.

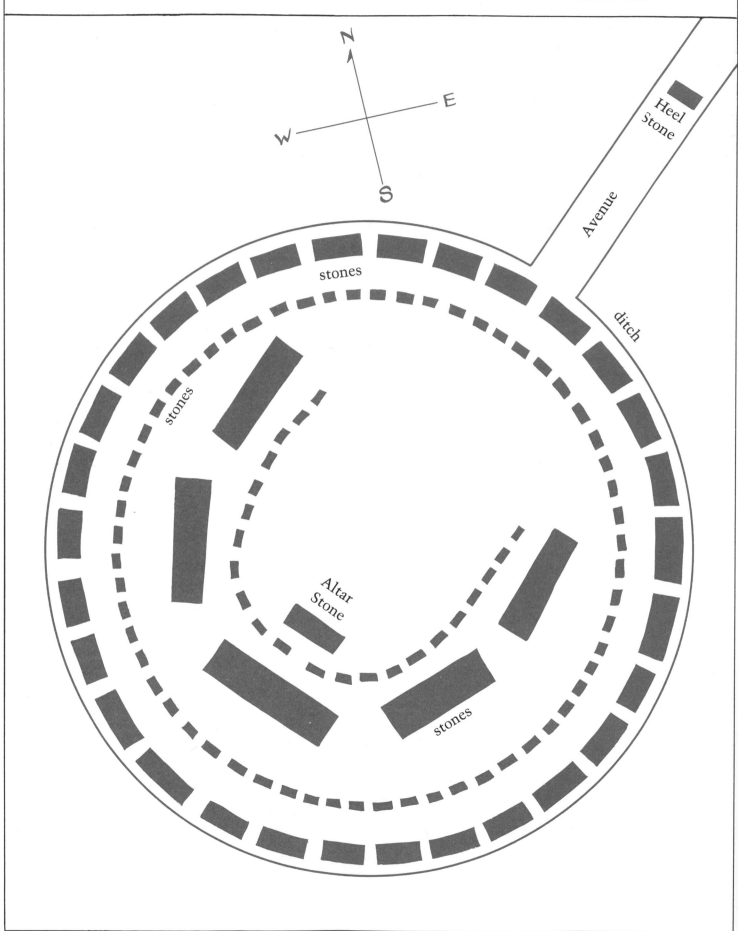

STONEHENGE AS A POSSIBLE CALENDAR

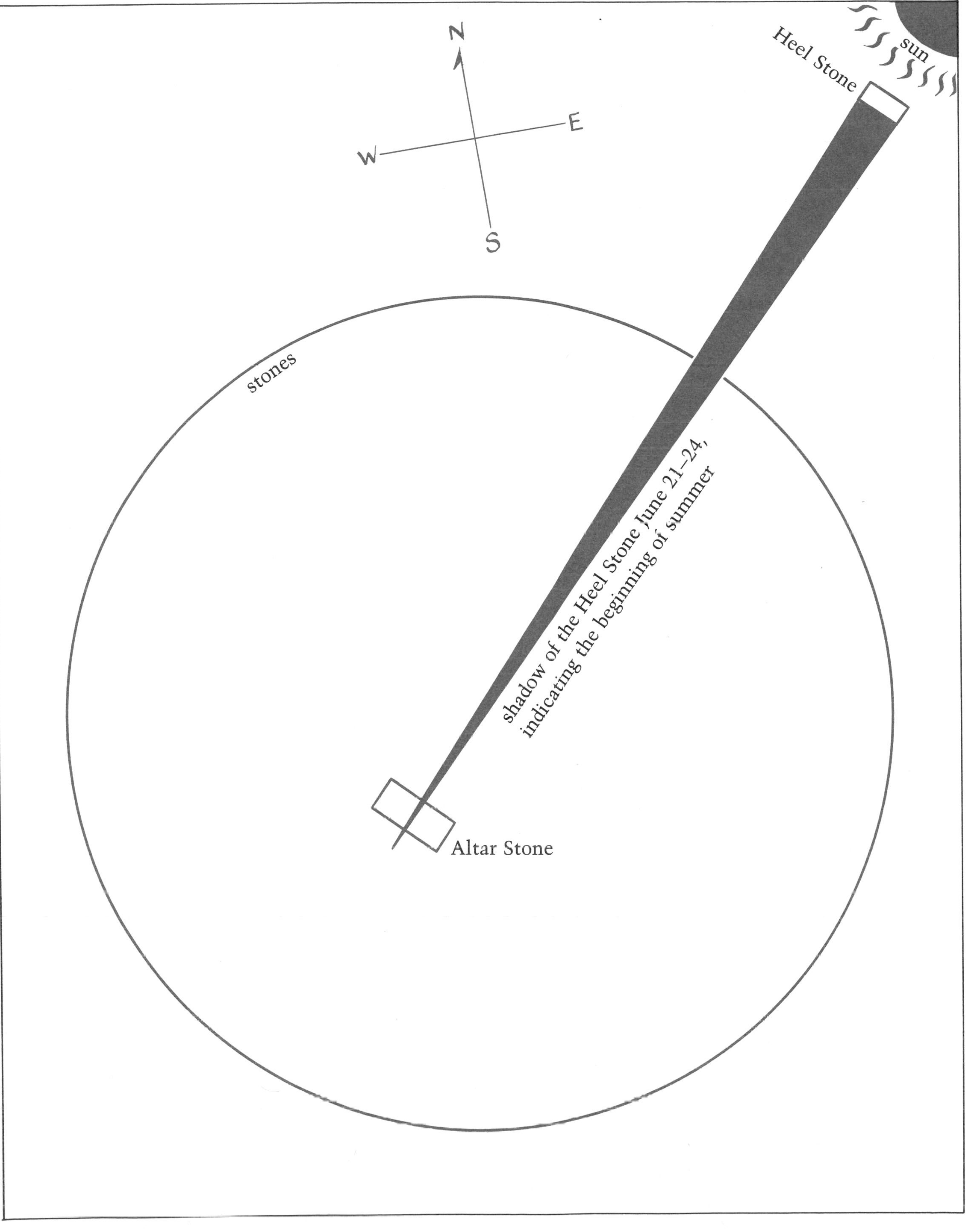

N

E

W

S

sun

Heel Stone

stones

shadow of the Heel Stone June 21–24, indicating the beginning of summer

Altar Stone

WORLD CALENDAR

Although the Gregorian calendar is sufficiently accurate, it is not perfect. And to many it is confusing. Since its construction more than 400 years ago, new calendars have been devised with the hope of improving on it. The most recent of these calendars, the one that offers the best chance for improvement over all calendars, is the World Calendar, originated by Elizabeth Achelis.

Designed in 1930, the best feature of the World Calendar is that it repeats itself exactly, year after year. Each year contains a basic 364 days. And every year begins on a Sunday, January 1. The year is divided into four quarters. Each quarter consists of 3 months having 91 days. The 91 days can be further described as being 3 months or 13 weeks. Each of the four quarters begins on a Sunday. Each of the four quarters ends on a Saturday.

To bring the 364-day World Calendar into line with the 365¼-day solar year, a non-numbered day, or Worldsday, would be added following every December 30. This day, W Day, would be a world-wide holiday. Also, following June 30 every fourth year, another non-numbered holiday would be added, Leap Year Day, or L Day. All holidays would fall on the same days every year. Christmas, for example, would always be on Monday. Such a simplified calendar would make it easy for the countries of the world to do business with one another. But it would be very difficult for different religious groups around the world to adapt to the World Calendar, since they use lunar calendars and strict rules to determine their holy days.

WORLD CALENDAR 1930

I

JANUARY

Sunday	1	8	15	22	29
Monday	2	9	16	23	30
Tuesday	3	10	17	24	31
Wednesday	4	11	18	25	
Thursday	5	12	19	26	
Friday	6	13	20	27	
Saturday	7	14	21	28	

FEBRUARY

Sunday		5	12	19	26
Monday		6	13	20	27
Tuesday		7	14	21	28
Wednesday	1	8	15	22	29
Thursday	2	9	16	23	30
Friday	3	10	17	24	
Saturday	4	11	18	25	

MARCH

Sunday		3	10	17	24
Monday		4	11	18	25
Tuesday		5	12	19	26
Wednesday		6	13	20	27
Thursday		7	14	21	28
Friday	1	8	15	22	29
Saturday	2	9	16	23	30

II

APRIL

Sunday	1	8	15	22	29
Monday	2	9	16	23	30
Tuesday	3	10	17	24	31
Wednesday	4	11	18	25	
Thursday	5	12	19	26	
Friday	6	13	20	27	
Saturday	7	14	21	28	

MAY

Sunday		5	12	19	26
Monday		6	13	20	27
Tuesday		7	14	21	28
Wednesday	1	8	15	22	29
Thursday	2	9	16	23	30
Friday	3	10	17	24	
Saturday	4	11	18	25	

JUNE

Sunday		3	10	17	24
Monday		4	11	18	25
Tuesday		5	12	19	26
Wednesday		6	13	20	27
Thursday		7	14	21	28
Friday	1	8	15	22	29
Saturday	2	9	16	23	30

Leap Year Day every fourth year   L

III					

JULY

Sunday	1	8	15	22	29
Monday	2	9	16	23	30
Tuesday	3	10	17	24	31
Wednesday	4	11	18	25	
Thursday	5	12	19	26	
Friday	6	13	20	27	
Saturday	7	14	21	28	

AUGUST

Sunday		5	12	19	26
Monday		6	13	20	27
Tuesday		7	14	21	28
Wednesday	1	8	15	22	29
Thursday	2	9	16	23	30
Friday	3	10	17	24	
Saturday	4	11	18	25	

SEPTEMBER

Sunday		3	10	17	24
Monday		4	11	18	25
Tuesday		5	12	19	26
Wednesday		6	13	20	27
Thursday		7	14	21	28
Friday	1	8	15	22	29
Saturday	2	9	16	23	30

IV					

OCTOBER

Sunday	1	8	15	22	29
Monday	2	9	16	23	30
Tuesday	3	10	17	24	31
Wednesday	4	11	18	25	
Thursday	5	12	19	26	
Friday	6	13	20	27	
Saturday	7	14	21	28	

NOVEMBER

Sunday		5	12	19	26
Monday		6	13	20	27
Tuesday		7	14	21	28
Wednesday	1	8	15	22	29
Thursday	2	9	16	23	30
Friday	3	10	17	24	
Saturday	4	11	18	25	

DECEMBER

Sunday		3	10	17	24
Monday		4	11	18	25
Tuesday		5	12	19	26
Wednesday		6	13	20	27
Thursday		7	14	21	28
Friday	1	8	15	22	29
Saturday	2	9	16	23	30

Worldsday every year   W

upper left, Chinese year; *upper right*, Julian *calends*; *lower left*, World leap year; *lower right*, Babylonian sun